What is clear in Jennifer O'Grady's daring second book of poems is that there are no limitations to this poet's imagination. Whether examining the most seemingly minuscule detritus—broken glass in a parking lot, or "a wind-stripped twig" in the mud—to the furthest universe ("the star in her bathroom mirror") and contemplation of mankind's gravest sins, O'Grady finds material. It is in the study of childhood aptitude for detachment. It is in the storm-torn pear tree, the alphabet, the garden in which she admires wildflowers with her mother. It is in back pages of the newspaper and the warrantee for a household appliance. O'Grady demonstrates the most admirable poetic dimensionality and ingenuity —breadth and depth, intellectual edge—with grace and levity to boot. Herein, find wonderment and horror entangling with wit and curiosity. *Exclusions & Limitations* is a grand poetic performance of a bright mind and marvelous, fine-tuned heart.

—ELIZABETH COHEN, Associate Professor of English at SUNY Plattsburgh and author of *Bird Light, The Family on Beartown Road,* and other books

PRAISE FOR EXCLUSIONS & LIMITATIONS

Underneath and sometimes literally between O'Grady's assured and subtly measured lines lurk dangers and "damages that may not be covered." Our lives are not conceived with warranties, and this poet views seemingly benign moments—a game of handball, a school bus departing, snapping a child's photo—with a keen maternal prescience that exposes them as fraught with foreboding. Moving edgily from catastrophe to the mysteriousness of love itself, O'Grady shows how to bear the unknowable and carry on in the midst of warnings in poems as classic as Cassandra and as contemporary as today's headlines.

—JEANNE MARIE BEAUMONT

Jennifer O'Grady's *Exclusions & Limitations* conjures the sort of dream world that follows you after you're awake. The speaker herself is numinous, recounting desire and its cost from some inevitable Purgatory. The collection's controlling metaphor is the mixed blessing of the Annunciation: "She will always be / at a disadvantage, needing proof, / needing pain to make everything / clear, and even the life / already growing inside her / is unbelievable, until it nearly / tears her apart." The carefully wrought sonic texture, the range of styles from prose poem to lyric, narrative to alliterative abecedarian induces an orchestral intensity. This is a book that refuses to go away after it's been placed back on the shelf.

—JOHN HOPPENTHALER

Always lyrically animated, the clear often-elegiac note struck in these poems signals O'Grady's wakefulness to the shifting light and shade of things. Here is a natural world brought to attention by the unsparing intensity of the poet's gaze. Whether listing the colors of cattle at pasture ("rust, tobacco and / ashen"), or observing goldfish in a pond ("quick bits/ of firelight, orange rind, / shrapnel, tiny meteors with / nowhere to fall"), O'Grady's exact, exacting language is always up to her descriptive, meditative task, while able also to bring to life a narrative-laden feminist landscape—familiar, mysterious, politically alert—as in the repeated evocation of famous painted Annunciations. Excavating moments in marriage and motherhood, she can also move to moments of prayer, the kind of courageous prayer these poems deserve: sharp-sighted, probing and pondering the ordinary adventure of life and its extraordinary hunger for what is to be loved, what is to survive: to find "gain not loss," even in what in any family is always passing. As testament to her whole enterprise, I would offer these lines:

> *Teach me to be patient,*
> *sleek jewel, brief one.*
>
> *Teach me to move*
> *in small spaces gracefully.*
>
> *Teach me limits, teach me*
> *to float. Teach me*
>
> *to decorate my life.*

As far as *Exclusions & Limitations* is concerned, O'Grady's prayer has been answered. Decisively.

—EAMON GRENNAN

EXCLUSIONS
& LIMITATIONS

Jennifer O'Grady

a plume editions book

AN IMPRINT OF MADHAT PRESS
ASHEVILLE, NORTH CAROLINA

MadHat Press
MadHat Incorporated
PO Box 8364, Asheville, NC 28814

The Library of Congress has assigned
this edition a Control Number of
2017913091

ISBN: 978-1-941196-56-4 (paperback)

Text by Jennifer O'Grady
Cover image by Marc Vincenz
Cover design by Marc Vincenz
Author photo by Deborah Lowery

Plume Editions
an imprint of MadHat Press
www.MadHat-Press.com

First Printing

EXCLUSIONS & LIMITATIONS

For Cameron and Chloe
And again, for Mark

TABLE OF CONTENTS

I

II

III

I

Shorn

Over roads without traffic, neat groves of grapefruit and honeybells
once dangling like unlit lanterns on palings now limbless, fallen or
   simply
gone; skimming fields of brief shining trailers like rows of scrubbed
   children

tucked in for the night; over branch-banged awnings and railings,
   small loved beds
of flooded begonias near holes where palmettos and lime trees once
   rose; then out
toward a colicky rocking ocean where whole schools of bluefish and
   fiddler crabs

lay motionless, coiled in gulfweed and tangle, the parking lot sifted
   with shattered glass.
Like a great bruised wing, a black wing covering the raveling line
of the landscape it traveled, swept into the rain-blurred yard where
   she ran

with the infant against her chest as wind without malice
grasped then plucked him—clotheslines snapping, tree roots vaulting—
a trail of ammonia still in the air, her arms like a room

with the roof blown off. Warm air expands, becomes lighter then rises
like a shriek or the bone-white *O* of the moon, and cool fills a void
where memory's heavy door won't shut, impossible

to fence as Virginia creeper, impossible to evade as our need to eat.

3

Exclusions & Limitations

The Company warrants that for a period from this date

> say, this hot, heavy day, air trapped between buildings,
> sun disappeared behind gray edemic clouds

this product will be free of defects in materials

> we gather our clothing
> descend the elevator

replacement will be made with a new or remanufactured part

> hail a taxi to bring us to the room
> where vows are made, fates will be altered

or a similar product of equal or greater value

> surrounded already by arrangements of blossoms
> the light, cool colors of detachment or disgust

What This Document Does Not Cover:

> or any such emotion we might hereby glimpse
> or unveil for each other as years pass, if only briefly

damage resulting from use or misuse

> I wear a gown the color and sheen
> of pearls, or the hidden undersides of their shells

or use contrary to operating instructions

> tread unsteadily in unfamiliar heels

Acts of God, such as fire, flood, or tornadoes

> sinking repeatedly into the red polyester
> runner, and having to be yanked out again

normal wear of parts not genuine

> you at the runner's end, tailored in black
> like the black of blindness, the black of deep sleep

limited again to the duration of the above

> our black and white costumes
> unattached to the softer, penetrable bodies

or incidental or consequential damages

> pulsing unstoppably, trailing the suspension bridge
> exposed to every weather over hypothermic waters

This is your exclusive warranty.

The Annunciation According to John Collier

For once, the angel
is film-star handsome,
more a gift than bearing a gift,
but alas, he is unattainable,
as angels are. The girl looks up

from her spark-red prayer book,
school dress billowing, shins
darkly naked, saddle shoes
firmly on her welcome mat.
The angel looks down

in modesty or submission, as if to say
I am less than you, which is true:
He cannot feel. And she is doomed
to be always looking at him,
the lily of purity

sprawling from its earthenware pot
between them. Or can he feel?
Is that why his face is shadowed,
tinged with a hint of mortal grief
for all the things he can never have—

this house on this street, a door
waiting to be opened—he leans toward it
as if staggered by the weight
of his wings. And she watches,
the prayer book lowered,

while she awaits illumination,
the child who will become
another man to leave her,
as the angel cannot do, and might wish
with all his heart he could.

Jennifer O'Grady

North Tower

When he looked up and saw
what he won't to this day talk about—

and what we won't to this day ask,
because the images it calls to mind

won't fit inside the mind's
dimness and limitations,

rationalizations and embarrassed
imagination, threatening

to spill and stain—his shirt
neatly buttoned and tucked—

so he rarely speaks,
except to say *sure* or *please*

pass the pepper we pass
in silence, hoping he'll request

nothing more of us.

Habitation

The long road south, pavement flat
and black as a dash without end, no signs,

no houses, heat like an unseen fog
and the sun a swollen crimson clot

above fields where frazzle-haired palm trees rose
sporadic and unwieldy, the miles

of pasture where cattle of every conceivable
color, rust, tobacco and ashen, nudged

and nursed their stumbling young,
heavy heads bowed to the ground.

And insects that crashed against windshield
so tiny no body was left behind.

Then a wooden shack where we stopped to pee
and the shock of iron-red flecks

against bowl, the water placid, unmoved.
There was hardly any pain.

What could we do but continue on
as scattered streetlamps gradually revealed

a landscape inhabited once again: the still
shuttered windows of bungalows pink

as scrubbed flesh, the small dark yards of abandoned
Bigwheels and plots of petunias or cukes,

the closed, expectant mailboxes
and the living already dead inside me.

Rabbit

There is something

                    not quite right

about this, the container

                    where he eats, sleeps, defecates, lies

with ruinous abandon

                    or in a dull stupor,

unable to tell us

                    which, if either;

amid wisps of hay, the now-

                    flowerless broccoli, stems

untouched, all we had

                    today in the fridge;

nibbling the pellets

                    of who knows what

we give him, chewing

                    the plastic bars

in periodic frustration

                    or lusty enjoyment,

long ungainly feet

                    stretched out behind him

not unlike the keychain

                    I had as a child,

good-luck charm, piece

                    of some unlucky being

I carried like a wounded

directionless compass,

exploring the sensation

of owning bone and fur

as we do now, owning

up to it at least, buying

his food, cage, toys

(mostly unused), treats,

him—

and where do we go

from here, where

does it lead us,

such captivity, if not

to the outer reaches

of ourselves,

where distance

or ambiguity

whisper that he is

much better off,

he is safe, while we watch

the moist protruding eyes

watch us: strange creatures

doing everything

and nothing at all.

Lot's Wife

Of course she will pause
to look back at what's familiar

after so much struggling uphill,
so much sinking in sand, the man

like a cattle prod urging her on.
And naturally, a male god

shuts her mouth forever,
no opportunity to argue or explain—

while somewhere, a woman
is tossed into fire

for wanting something more
than her arranged life contains, pain

into greater pain, flesh into stone.
The husband and the one

they call God will leave her,
hardened and abandoned

to the pecking of birds
who come for the bright salt—

yet another sacrifice—
unaware of her pointing hand

mapping the way home
for centuries of women.

Westside Women's Pavilion

I remember a door, white door. Handprints on it.

This is not good news, she said.

A waiting room, everyone young,
everyone almost a child, and me
almost dead. Well, something
inside me dead. That much I knew.

> *We don't do this in our office,* she said
> and handed me a shiny pink brochure,
> one corner gone like a bite.

A paper gown, paper slippers. I thought:
How will I walk without tearing them?

> *Sorry,* she said. *Sorry,*
> she said, then smiled.

In the room a girl, fourteen perhaps,
looked at me. *Don't worry,*
she said. *It's not bad. They're nice.*
I looked at her; she looked at me,
her pupils lit by the filthy fluorescent
hanging like a casket from the dropped ceiling
covered in dull white fire-retardant
sound-reduction tiles.

> *At least we know it can happen,* she said,
> *It's conceivable.* No pun intended.

Next, they said and she went,
sucking a lollipop.

> *See you in another six weeks,* she said
> as she closed the door.

Next, they said
to the living and the dead.

Flight

I

          toward the barbed-wire fence,
the children saw and closed in. He galloped

unseeing, trusting his instincts and legs,
nostrils flaring, chestnut coat foamy with sweat.

What happened next we can only imagine:
The road beyond the high wire beckoned

like a river far below the jumper,
glittering in day's last light.

Midflight he lost his balance and pitched,
tumbling onto the brambled wire, the ground

hollowing where he fell. And beyond them
the occasional, rushed car, vanishing.

II

          with something so small:
A boy drops a glass and his mother slaps him

in the unflinching light of the kitchen. He didn't
mean it, perhaps he was in a hurry:

It was early September, still warm.
Through the open window, beyond the orchard

the distant, relentless *thwack* of a bat
and someone is running as cheers go up.

He can feel his legs take him over the bases
then back toward home where the girls are calling,

buds of their breasts nudging hand-me-down T-shirts,
long hair swinging in the breeze.

III
                    and others, leaders;
because the boy could hear the girls

cheering him on, even in his sleep;
because of the lush, sweet grass of the pasture

(the invisible pattern of a ball field
waiting to be mapped out);

because when the ball fell into the pasture
and the boy climbed over the gate to retrieve it

the horse jealously charged him and for a moment,
he was afraid; because the horse was curried

and stroked, because somebody loved it
as one would love a child.

IV

       until he lay still
as nightfall, still as the lifeless pond

beyond the schoolyard, where no one dared go.
They beat him until they were breathless

from the effort, until he could no longer see
and stayed there, lying by the side of the road,

flung down like a heavy branch in wind
in autumn, pressed into the soundless earth

edged with weeds, sprouting crimson clover.
It would take a day before he was found,

chestnut coat covered thinly with dust
tossed up by the tires of speeding trucks.

V

       standing near the kitchen door
as the blossom-white, irretrievable milk

flows over linoleum, glass at his feet
in jagged fragments and his mother slaps him

as cheers go up. He watches her turn
to the counter, the muscles of her back

19

Jennifer O'Grady

like tree roots working to surface,
the silence between them taut as a road,

pocked and empty, coated with dust.
In the faraway orchard the girls are calling:

their voices slip away over the grass
like lost chances, a thing of the past.

Two Birds Mating In A Rhododendron Bush

If only it could be
as simple as this:

      flicker of gray wings

between green
egg-shaped leaves,

      branches unbloomed,

almost prepared
to increase themselves,

      leaves fluttering too

but tethered
in the still wet garden,

      the two of them

unashamed
and unafraid,

      temporarily
      and partially sheltered

here

      beneath the unattached sky.

Jennifer O'Grady

All Souls

*… All Souls Day (November 2ⁿᵈ), when the Catholic world remembers the
dead who are in Purgatory.*

I

First the vial, then the needle,
then the instructions

      The clanging Campanile bell
      signals transition, its jangled harmony

      flung like pieces of shattered mosaic
      high above the *palazzi* windows

      shuttered like so many indifferent ears—

the instructions having to be
repeated again

      enviable ocher and terra cotta,
      lemon, emerald and pistachio greens,

      stones the color of old melons
      or tangerines left on a shelf too long

then the images, the egg waxing
like an inner moon

      or pumpkin-colored, like the market's *zucca*
      split, its insides glistening—

pinched fold of puckered thigh
then the prick of the needle,

the almost invisible
hole it left, closing

    all else seems gray, the glazed ash
    of doorways, the dull dun of railings

    arching above bridges and beyond
    paint-peeling walls

check calendar, plan the coupling

    the gray murk of so many
    overwhelmed canals

blood test like a form
of injury, a form of hope

    and sometimes white, startling
    as a pigeon's underwings

and once more, the bleeding
out of all hope

II

Rain, the endless confetti of rain

    Then flight, the desire
    to rest, to forget

pearling hair, clinging
in lucid bits to your earlobes

as if we could, our thoughts
now hidden from each other

pink as the market's *gambaretti*
layered in crushed ice, sepia-stained

submerged like the Zattere
washed by the tide—

a flayed lemon sole
revealing its tangle of pale-pink veins

we walk over wooden planks
meant to protect us

beneath a red frescoed arch

skimming puddles
as a splintered sun breaks through

then retreats again,
not unlike you

plaster the color of old biscuits
or peaches left on a shelf too long

a black *traghetto* plows the canal, leaving
a wake that heals itself

the moment it's broken

round a corner, a small pile
of powdered blue pigment

abandoned by an artist
in the midst—

III

Night and Gritti's marble terrace,
rain slapping flagstones and plastic chairs

    Your *where?*
    my *anywhere*

    older than I am

a thumbprint moon's
veiled hide-and-seek behind clouds

    your *now?*
    my *no, not yet it's too soon*

we ride the *vaporetto,*
hardly anyone on it

    unexpectedly
    you take my hand

past boarded windows
and damp gilded rooms

Jennifer O'Grady

in our room we scrabble
for purchase with each other

forsaken housing
rocked by the tides

bodies aligned
briefly, heedless

of what we might
make or lose—

rain rinsing buildings
or wearing them down

for a moment,
then I lie back

you extinguish the swirling
blown-glass lamp

feeling the ceaseless
sway later,

when I close my eyes

II

How to Clean Practically Anything

Yes, housework can be a chore

A day, a day rinsed free of night

everyone enjoys a clean and orderly home

table wiped clear of crumbs and spills

the best way to do the maximum amount
of work, without becoming overwhelmed

floor swept, dustpan emptied into plastic
bags placed inside sealed metal cans

is to perform it in a systematic fashion

dishwasher emptied, opaque and stainless

blot the stain, wipe away any residue

whites now sorted, his socks, his shirts
old egg-yolk yellow under the arms

try these to ensure results
reward your efforts:

his underwear, the boxers faded and frayed
repeating their pattern of angular hearts

be sure to remove any hooks or weights

> their scattered and miniature x's and o's
> openings measured for admission or exit

don't overload the machine, and remember

> his colors tangling in a tossed-off pile
> of mostly darks, mostly blacks and blues

fabric becomes much heavier when wet

> while here and there a spring green
> a tremulous yellow

protect from strong sunlight
and abrasive objects

> a newborn pink, streak of surprisingly deep red

warning: damages may not be covered

> like fresh blood, a raw and unsutured cut

try a product that claims to hide
surface scratches

> to be rinsed and wrung, dried and folded and piled
> into the thing we call a long marriage

if the marks have darkened
use a sharp knife

     these daily removals, these many attempts
     to wipe clean the counter the table the slate

if the burn is deep use filler
smoothing it to match the surface

     the windows now free of fingerprints and smears
     as if there were no glass no barrier no space

work carefully to avoid
damaging the paint

     in which to revisit your own faint reflection

this coating should last for years

Jennifer O'Grady

End Of Summer

Everywhere, death
assumes an innocent expression:

that sweetgum branch overhanging the walk,
gifting its shade like a deep elixir,

now seems a weight about to plummet
precisely on the spot where my child digs

with a wind-stripped twig in the clinging mud,
and even the twig's lone leaf now holds,

to my eyes, sharp, ineradicable dangers—
until the bus arrives, its engine rumbling

time. I try to hold him
but he pulls away, climbs on

without a wave, balancing
as the bee-colored vehicle disappears

in a sunrise too bright to see into.

Annunciation

In Fra Angelico's fresco, Mary's
unremarkable and still, a girl
like any other, while the angel
in balloon-red frock leans toward her, smiling.

Mary looks away. There is no going back
except for the angel, whose peacock-feather wings
in earth tones with strokes so realistic
you can nearly feel them at fingertips

softly rigid, are pointing
away from her, as if to indicate escape.
But there is no escape: Her life will become
one lone monument to sorrow. While the angel

who casts no shadow, who will never be anyone's
lover or mother, smiles as one
forever unencumbered, and like a child
he's enigmatic and symbolic, always

just about to leave.

Jennifer O'Grady

Alphabet for the Stay-At-Home Parent

An abacus arrived at abeyance.
Bobbled-headed. Bitter but bright.
Claustrophobic cacophony. Causing crushing.
Death-defying. Dyspepsia. Dustpan.
Easy exercise. Enormous errors.
Fossilization. Feeling fortunate. Fantasy.
Goddammit/gosh goodness. Gaffes galore.
Hate hamburgers, hate hot dogs. Hysterectomy.
Igloos. Idolatry. Identity crisis.
Juice. Jousting. Joy.
Karate kicks. Knackered.
Lapsing laughter. Lacking like.
Me. Mine. Mentholated.
No!
Opining. Obviously ordinary.
Polemical Pop Tarts.
Quiet!
Ridiculous rooster-rising. Rage.
Sorry, so sorry. Sitting. Sobbing. Silence.
Tremendous theater-of-the-trite.
Underneath umbrellas. Uneasy urges.
Virulent vigilance. Victorious vetoing.
Why?
Xylophone-pounding X-chromosome. X-rated (e)xpletives.
Yoked. Yielding. Yachtsman. Yearning.
Zoo. Zoloft. Zanzibar. Zen. Zenith.

Flag

Oh Flag waving at my neighbor's door
are you beckoning or warning Oh Flag

dangling like a tired wing this hushed
midwinter morning against a bordered

metal sky threatening to snow Old Glory
your colors were once bright weren't they

the soft cloth clean as new snow
or unrolled bandages

the deep blue promise of a summer dusk
studded with stars now dim as deepest night

the once ardent red
dull as old scars Oh flag

twisting over doorways shut and bolted
inhabitants waving good-bye

to kids in private schools kids in public schools
privatized with fences with hedges high windows

that hold back a sky swollen with snow
who will never know the cold

shock of bullets the embrace
of clean white bandages Old Glory

Jennifer O'Grady

your brothers stand sentry all around town
twitch in the dull midwinter light:

red stripes blue fields long soiled whites
like columns of newsprint

where the names of the dead
in fading five-point type peep out

to wave one last good-bye before
we fold them and put them away

Tomorrow

My son comes out of school in the late afternoon
       inflated by winter layers, looking for someone
       who wants him—not me, of course, I am

old hat, yesterday's leavings—someone like him
       but no one is quite like him, no one
       wants him right now, this very minute which is

everything, all we are ever meant to see
       and he sees it, his yesterdays and tomorrows
       not yet fogging up the windows

where he waits, the winter
       making ghosts of his breath
       while his body produces more and more, each one

floating away to nowhere—
       everyone rushes past, everyone looks beyond
       where he stands in green winter jacket and cap

rigid, not wanting to miss
       the slightest possibility, but nobody sees him
       as they rush toward each other

making matches, twinning themselves,
       their bodies like his, backpacks
       and sneakers like his as they fall

into Lexuses, Buicks and Fords,
       doors opening remotely, allowing them access,
       voices now muffled, doors sliding into place

and in another moment they are gone, nothing
　　　　but exhaust smoke lingering
　　　　then vanishing too

while he waits there in silence
　　　　and his insulating jacket
　　　　almost glowing, almost emerald

in the dissipating light,
　　　　little breath-ghosts still being produced
　　　　and moving away, the cap half-shadowed,

face almost shapeless, almost blending
　　　　with the night where he waits
　　　　motionless and filled

with the beautiful boundless certainty
　　　　that tomorrow, everything
　　　　will change.

The Annunciation According to Henry Ossawa Tanner

This one's mere light:
insubstantial, always moving.
How are we to trust it?
And indeed, the Virgin
stays on her white-trussed bed,
hands clasped, hunched
away from it.

Called as she is, singled out,
as she is, her expression
cannot be called happy—
eyes skeptical, forehead slightly
creased in a frown—
while the column of light
looms in her windowless chamber,
limbless and featureless.
How are we to believe it?

She will always be
at a disadvantage, needing proof,
needing pain to make everything
clear, and even the life
already growing inside her
is unbelievable, until it nearly
tears her apart. Until then,
any gift appears transparent,
liable to exit, like light,
without a trace.

Jennifer O'Grady

This is her real cross:
bearing the loss
of happiness

to understand what it was.

Ride

I cannot help her
and she knows it, as she climbs
on again and again,

the too-big boy's helmet
with its lightning bolt a reflection
of the lowering sun.

Some things will be harder
and some, for her, easier:
the way she might learn

to toss hair back, or a barely there
layer of red lipstick, lips curved
outward, like a hook. She will learn

not from me but from existence,
as she learns to climb on
then fall off again,

body hitting pavement
with the least amount of resistance,
making no mark

as she learns to make her mark.
These things will happen
in the distance, where she rides

away from me, battered
blue helmet still askew,
her lovely face leading,

tangled braids splaying in the wind.

Nothing Could Stop It

not the swift spoked wheels passing the scarlet maples,
not the bent crabapple's thick arthritic boughs,
not the bold crows scattering like ash
when the boys ran from their hiding place

(a new detached garage); not the school uniform,
not even her mother
waiting just down the road at home
while the sun, the only witness, fell behind a hedge.

Oranges or cupcakes, water or chocolate milk,
pleasure versus health, she wondered as she stood
and her child was pulled from the pink bike, thrown
to the grass—handfuls up her nose and pushed

down her throat, the inescapable earth
clinging to its roots the last flavor she tasted—
spokes spinning on still bike,
her own movements done as they ran

toward homes where other mothers stood,
just as my door opens and my daughter rushes in.
Is it true? she asks, and I begin, then see her face—
then *No, no,* I say, *no, it's all wrong.*

Jennifer O'Grady

Fireflies

In July when the children
        are fast asleep and day begins
its shading to dusk,

            from the shelter of our
       screened porch we watch
         their brief

transformations: small orbs
        blinking like unintelligible signals
above the groundcover

          then vanishing, only
     to appear somewhere else:
          beneath, say, the arms

of the ornamental pear
        or over by the broken gate
no one can enter,

          their cold light
     strange proclamations of love
          or hunger, faint sparks

pricking the darkness
        filled with its tense
promise of rain, invisible clouds

          holding it in.
   Who really knows
          another, what each

is capable of
    if the moment is ripe?
When day comes and we

       can no longer see them
    they are there still,
       unaccounted for

       in the outer all-encompassing light.

Jennifer O'Grady

Photograph

He refuses to be in it, my son, here, the moment
I aim to freeze with my new Apple camera,

instrument of halting time as slight
as my palm while the rogue cloud barreling overhead

threatens to ruin my light. But he won't
come into view, as if he already

resents, at eight, how energy bends
when it meets with any obstruction,

or senses whatever image I catch
is merely a hint of where he'll be, shadow

of where he's been. And as if he can pity
how much I want to keep him

fixed in my limited range of sight
he edges into the almost gone light,

permitting one small reduction of himself
while I point my lens toward his fading form,

saying *don't move, don't move, now smile.*

Dusk

Down the street a cemetery
        stood side by side with a factory

against whose wall we hit balls, not
        dressed-up tennis balls, courts

a phenomenon in Queens, but
        naked spaldeens, rough pink

handheld nearly celestial spheres
        at night, when the factory was shut.

What kind of factory we never knew
        or cared, never seeing a soul

enter its plate-glass doors, their momentum
        for daytime, the grownup world.

The dim half-moon of a streetlamp gave us
        just enough light to see our wall,

the patch of scratchy sidewalk,
        our hands striking the ball.

The stones of the cemetery crowded together
        like elders before an impending doom.

What they tried to tell us we couldn't hear
        or didn't want to, the static summer air

broken only by the streetlamp's hum
       harmonized by the deep percussive

thunk of our ball as we sent it away
       and always the wall returned it, and one

by one the distant voices of our mothers,
       still traveling like light from long-dead stars,

calling us home to bed.

Stars

As long as it remains chilled and the shell closed, the oyster can survive transport. *Did you know it's a long way to Tipperary?* Then: *How long till we're there?* "There" being not the pool but a dental office, she having no idea a cavity will be filled. The dentist pretends it's a star—*getting a star on her tooth.* She picks out the "glitter" color, aqua like her shorts, then sits, the padded chair too big for her as the drill goes in, following instructions far more complex than mine, all in expectation of a star she can't see.

I remember being seven, the priest telling me to confess or I couldn't be "absolved," his word meaning nothing to me other than a soft whisper drawing me in.

We'll have oysters tonight but she won't eat them—*too slippery* she says and I have to agree, yet with no sharp edges, nothing visible to harm. The things we omit from our bedtime stories: guns, famine, Dachau, the little boy cut up and put in someone's refrigerator when all he wanted was to find his way home. Maybe Tipperary lies in what is now the far north and is rarely visited, bombs still planted there like flowers or corn. Gloves are recommended for the opening of oysters—*shucking* it's called, to strip or peel off—while open shells signify danger: *Discard.*

Later she'll look for the star in her bathroom mirror, mouth pulled open to its widest extent while outside, distant chips of starlight appear. When he pressed me, the priest, I told him I'd lied. They told them a long journey but it was nine miles from Munich, nearly the distance she goes each day to camp, waving.

Contact

I

Used to indicate position above and supported by or in contact with

> *A two-year-old girl was beaten to death*

the object affected by actual, perceptible action

> *apparently because she would not stop crying.*

the object of an action moving toward or against it

> *Asked if he was subject to angry outburst,*

a corrective taken or undertaken routinely

> *a woman claiming to be a sister of the defendant*

concerning and to the disadvantage of

> *said, "Only when somebody wears his shirt."*

without stopping; continuously

II

A common pattern is to view especially loud and urgent cries as the ones signaling pain. Should this happen, the seeds for inadvertent shaping of screaming are in place.

III

Asked what she meant, she said, "You know, if you put on my pants I get angry."

IV

In the police report it was noted

into a distance of space or time

that the pants (size 2) and shirt (also size 2)

extending or branching out from

were clean and consistent with normal growth

to be lesser or fewer

while the pattern of injuries

not taking place; canceled

indicated a one-time occurrence

V

Studies involving the extinction method show that young children have a higher aptitude for detachment—in other words, they eventually stop making all sound. Whether this inhibits response in later years is something yet to be found.

VI

To shape or break by repeated blows

    metal into a dagger

To mix with an instrument

    two eggs cracked in a bowl

To flap, as wings. So as to produce a signal. To make inarticulate sounds or calls

    used of an animal

To defeat or subdue, as in a contest. To hunt through underbrush in search of game. To beg for

    cry forgiveness

To emit sound when struck

Like an Ear

We walk a littered verge dividing field from street—two small figures, one large figure— aiming for a car crouched in the dark like a stalking animal. The moon's lost, hidden by swollen clouds—I stumble and keep going. One grabs the other's ball or doll, clashing as old as time but tonight I snap, manhandle them in, flip the ignition, stomp pedal—and only then discover that one isn't buckled. I brake and reach for the backseat, skin already rigid, teeth clenched. They are old enough to know better—I justify mid-shriek—the sound shocking even me. Their eyes are wide and distant as Jupiter's moons. We drive in astral silence while I steer us around each shadowy corner, even the trees turning away from me. Sudden brights fill the rearview mirror, making me squint in the unwanted light and still the silence, another kind of taking away, pervades the interior. We will travel that way for a long, long time. The moon gleams like an ear scrubbed clean.

III

Pear in Storm

It couldn't withstand the riptide wind
       descending like Nemesis,

heavy rain-battered branches shearing off
       at the peak of pressure, toppled, leaving

its own bark skinned, heartwood exposed
       and never again the same. We mourn

what it was as we mourn ourselves
       falling that way, stripping for each other

even though damage is imminent, inevitable
       as bitter wind or rain, nothing

forcing us through that drowned night
       but fear and sheer wanton flight.

Jennifer O'Grady

The Annuniciation According to Tissot

Here Mary sits, figured
in malleable water

and fugitive pigments,
head drooping, possibly

asleep, practically straitjacketed,
the white robes so dense

no part of her is visible
except for one palm upturned, empty,

the face we can barely see.
Surprisingly, the angel appears

to be female, swathed in long feathers,
tapered hands raised in greeting or prevention,

for who but a woman could understand
the bleeding, the separation, the lingering

after one's child is gone, nothing but spirit
left to leave you and a straitjacket

might be better than this: seeing
the life you created beat out of him, shattered

until there is nothing to hold, nothing
to keep you from being alone.

The angel with her far-reaching vision knows all
and has come this time perhaps in warning:

wake up, wake up, it's not too late.
But Mary sleeps on, seemingly

drugged, forever fading, heedless
of the urgent message she bears,

the one that will spoil her life.

Jennifer O'Grady

The Trainer, After

They warned me such a creature
would never understand any attempt
to caress it, for instinct
is what it knows, which is inherently

nothing: no choice, only deep
blind need, the body's
Mack-truck-like existence. Mother
called almost every morning,

Father wouldn't speak of the fear
that ate at him daily, but didn't need to:
It was all there, swimming
in his eyes. Tilikum

circled me that day, just a day
like any other, blue, clouds moving too fast.
Yet there was something, some energy
I chose to ignore, wanting only

to encourage him, and when he opened
his jaw I could see
the end there, black, deep, moving
too fast. Tell Father

I'm sorry. Tell Mother
not to weep, for this
was my choice too:
giving my whole self in love.

Museum Garden

We enter a painted gate, my mother and I
as we wait for the others, and stroll its perimeter
bordered by heirloom flowers, their handwritten signs—
Feverfew, Sweet William, Canterbury Bells—

blurred by years of bright summer sun.
Others we find too difficult to read, so we wonder
what they're called, reeling out our small talk
as shadows slip over the old stone wall.

My mother is tired, although she won't admit it,
and though I want her to sit, she continues to walk—
neither of us wants it, yet neither will give
the other clear signs of her innermost thoughts

and it has been this way, probably,
as long as I can remember. *I remember*
a bench like that she says, from long ago,
and though memory can't tell her if it was

yellow or white, it doesn't matter, the thought
makes her smile to herself. We continue
past *Scarlet Runner, Throatwort, Honesty*
and other blossoms whose names I can't make out,

her step slowing somewhat as she looks at the bench
she refuses to sit on, and still I say nothing.
This is what it means to love someone: to pretend
that what we can't see is what's really there,

or something similar—that what we now miss
isn't missing—and if we look away
we might envision what's gone, as my mother
can read more markers than I

by ignoring their wobbly, sun-faded script.
Then we go on, past *Sweet Rocket,*
Golden Glow and *Thyme* and exit
the same way we came in, the distant

church bells chiming down the hours.

Man Keeps Eighty Sheep in His House, Authorities Say

yet who can say
how love must be bestowed,
        or where lie its limits? What to one

    is a rare treat, Sunday
bounty, is to another
        waste or grief,

    the remains of it
still leaking on the plate,
        wet as the pink and red

    markered hearts
our daughter scrawls and thrusts at us
        whenever we pass by,

    their borders unable to hold
so much color, the color itself so saturated
        it bleeds, nearly destroying

    the paper underneath,
her love for us vast
        and uncontained, so that even

    when we pass her by,
unglancing, it is there still,
        brimming and spilling

    from her eyes.
And though we might take
        her hearts and lose them,

absentmindedly placing them
in the recycling bin,
               who is to say

the giving's unwise, the gift
unneeded? Who can live,
               love gone,

in the wake of its absence?
For aren't we all
               always in the end

like that: bleating
and bleeding
               for love.

Goldfish

Sealed in a glass womb,
voiceless, useless as a new penny,

your few swift moves rehearsed to perfection
even when no one is knocking or watching,

suspended, always looking out.

*

In Matisse's several, barely perceptibly
different paintings, four of them huddle

in the depthless perspective of a crystal canister
framed by a profusion of buoyant pink flowers,

sea-green leaves and the turquoise
arm of a wicker chair. The fish

are like wedges of fresh blood
in a split lip, and open-mouthed

as if about to sing.

*

In Fuzhou, farmers scoop you
from concrete ponds, quick bits

of firelight, orange rind, shrapnel,
tiny meteors with nowhere to fall.

Jennifer O'Grady

The glimmering end
of a cigarette

burning itself out.

*

Once I was taken to a local fair
where Ferris wheel and tilt-a-whirl, clockwise

and continual, spun brightly against the sky.
I won a goldfish the color of the setting sun.

Dreaming perhaps of some riverbed
deep in its past, my fish kept drifting

into the invisible walls of its bowl,
and I stretched fingers all the way around it

so he'd know where his world ended
and mine began. Next morning

he lay at the shadowy bottom,
a spent balloon, finally

having burst all limits.

*

Teach me to be patient,
sleek jewel, brief one.

Teach me to move
in small spaces gracefully.

Teach me limits, teach me
to float. Teach me

to decorate my life.

Jennifer O'Grady

Addition

As in enlarging or expanding,
as in piecing together

       He sits at the brand-new kitchen table
       in dwindling light, a flat screen before him

erasing what was
to make something new

       adolescent fingers tapping the keyboard,
       summoning scaffolds of symbols and signs

concrete then rubble,
foundation then floor

       as in growth, as in cells
       pulled out of thin air

as in two feet becoming
four, eating up the yard

       rough drafts of muscle
       supporting the bone

on the blueprints there was no
yard, only lines

       the face already leaner, nearly
       unrecognizable

only white space
where a yard would be

      the legs longer, faster
      for walking away

the wraparound porch
like a formal embrace:

      Look what I've done, he says
      beaming, and I look

as in gain, not loss

      then he stands and goes,
      leaving me to sit

not loss, not loss

      in this gleaming expanse,
      this now-finished space

        To start over click *CLEAR*

Jennifer O'Grady

Visitors

Having just arrived, we are walked down a moonless
boardwalk cutting through seagrape and orchids
and whatever wasn't lost to hurricanes or frost
is dim and trembling in the cool night air, then

down to a beach that erodes each winter, shifting
with our weight as we step on it, still warm, and go
to the place where water touches land, soft
and mutable shoreline of this barrier island

he has chosen to live on, against our better judgment.
The ocean waves roar like wild things freed, pounding
the sand and washing away footprints, anonymous
leavings of anonymous lives, while my father,

a little stooped now, stands apart, as if waiting
for our approval, or merely thinking his own thoughts.
A huddled black shape, blacker than the night
so we know it's really there, with the clear silhouette

of a pelican's bill a few yards away
sits motionless as a tourist taking in the view
but mixed-up, here at the wrong time of day, and
Don't go any closer my father says, for somehow

he knows this bird is no visitor but one
who's come to take in his last view of earth,
the place where desire or memory brought him
and from which he must know he won't rise again,

and we stand awhile, marveling at his perfect calm,
the near-regal set of the old weathered bill
that points straight ahead toward an indistinct space
through which we can hear the rush of each wave

coming closer every moment, as if they can't wait
to reach and carry him back to their home
and he waits, as if it's his purpose and choice—
then my father shepherds us all away,

moving more slowly but just as determined,
and we step on the boardwalk and follow him back
through stubborn survivors of wind and loss
to the place where he knows he belongs.

Jennifer O'Grady

Steer Flees Slaughter and Is Last Seen Going Thataway

They must have felt at least
a splinter of regret
that drowsy morning, one split second

collapsing open like a slit throat
when they realized what they'd done—
the steel door slammed back,

the stall that should have restrained him
strangely unlocked and gaping.
Or a moment of reproach

when the tire sank
and the missing jack was back in the truck
where he stood, absorbing

the migrants' cries
beyond the slaughterhouse walls.
Was there an instant

when they could almost taste him—
Bolognese simmering
in its lidded pot, patties

clenched between toasted buns
or red flesh sliced thin and salted?
There was a moment when,

despite themselves, they made no move
to stop him but stood
the way one stands in a sudden rain:

furious at first, then surrendering
to the lawless, spreading warmth of it,
the extravagance of its force.

Let's say they savored
their last, swift vision:
two sleek tapering pennants of bone

severing air and pointing up
toward a brightening sky, that wild expanse
where a world of limitlessness begins,

and the ungovernable light.

Jennifer O'Grady

Anniversary

In twin chairs by the lakeside tonight
we've watched day's last light

spread like a bright blush over the treetops
past the point where cabins stand

abandoned, sealed against winter.
In the middle distance the island floats,

fading. There alone the wild blueberries
hang like unmarked globes over water

separating shore from shore.
Why they grow there but not here

puzzles, like love or the coming bereavements
of autumn, or rumors of empty, drifting skiffs.

For now at least the island remains
part and not part of the unknowing night

as we are to each other
island and mainland, ship and shore,

a familiar place; a mystery.

NOTES

"Exclusions & Limitations": italicized language is adapted from a standard product warranty.

"The Annunciation According to John Collier": John Collier is an American artist.

"How to Clean Practically Anything": italicized language is adapted from the book of the same title, published by Consumer Reports.

"The Annunciation According to Henry Ossawa Tanner": Henry Ossawa Tanner (1859–1937) was the first African-American painter to become internationally recognized.

"Contact": italicized language in sections I and III is adapted from *The New York Times*.

"*Man Keeps Eighty Sheep in His House, Authorities Say*" is the title of a widely disseminated news article.

"The Annunciation According to Tissot": James Tissot (1836–1902) was a French painter and illustrator.

"*Steer Flees Slaughter and Is Last Seen Going Thataway*" is the title of an article in *The New York Times*.

ACKNOWLEDGMENTS

Many thanks to the editors and staff of these publications, in which the following first appeared (some in different versions or with different titles):

Connotation Press: An Online Artifact: "All Souls," "Annunciation," "The Annunciation According to Tissot," "Exclusions & Limitations"

Cultural Weekly: "Westside Women's Pavilion," "Rabbit"

The Florida Review: "Goldfish"

Green Mountains Review: "Stars"

Literary Mama: "Addition," "Alphabet for the Stay-at-Home Parent," "Like an Ear"

The New Republic: "Two Birds Mating in a Rhododendron Bush"

One: "Anniversary"

Plume: "Fireflies," "Visitors"

The Plume Anthology of Poetry 5: "*Man Keeps Eighty Sheep in His House, Authorities Say*"

Poetry: "Habitation"

The Recorder: "Shorn," "*Steer Flees Slaughter and Is Last Seen Going Thataway*"

Red Truck Review: "The Annunciation According to John Collier," "Lot's Wife," "Pear in Storm"

Salamander: "Dusk"

Saranac Review: "Museum Garden," "The Trainer, After"

Seneca Review: "Contact"

Southwest Review: "How to Clean Practically Anything"

Tar River Poetry: "Photograph," "Tomorrow"

"How to Clean Practically Anything" also appeared on *Poetry Daily.*

"Flight" received a Billee Murray Denny Poetry Award and was published by Lincoln College in *The Denny Poems.*

"Flag" received Honorable Mention for the James J. Nicholson Political Poetry Prize.

"Dusk" and "Tomorrow" were nominated for Pushcart Prizes.

My enormous thanks to April Ossman and Wyn Cooper for their encouragement and close readings of these poems, and to Marc Vincenz and Danny Lawless for their support of this work. To my loving family and the many friends (too many to list here) who provided feedback on these poems over the years, my eternal gratitude.

ABOUT THE AUTHOR

JENNIFER O'GRADY is a poet and playwright. Born to an Italian-American mother and an Irish father, she grew up in New York City and earned a BA from Vassar, where she won awards for her poetry, and an MFA from Columbia University. She is the author of *White*, winner of the Mid-List Press First Series Award for Poetry and a Greenwall grant from The Academy of American Poets. Her poems have been taught, anthologized, set to music, and featured in *Harper's*, *The New Republic*, *The Writer's Almanac* with Garrison Keillor, *Poetry*, *Poetry Daily*, *American Poetry: The Next Generation* and numerous other places. Her poems have garnered a Billee Murray Denny Award, a W.K. Rose Fellowship, and Pushcart Prize nominations, among other honors. Her plays include *Charlotte's Letters* (The Irish Repertory Theatre's New Works Series and Semifinalist for the O'Neill Center's National Playwrights Conference and BETC's Generations Award); *Paranormal Love* (Winner: Manhattan Theatre Works NewBorn Festival; Finalist: NEWvember New Play Festival); *Ellery* (selected for *The Best Women's Stage Monologues* 2017); *Quasars* (selected for *The Best Women's Stage Monologues* 2014 and *Best Contemporary Monologues for Women 18–35*); *Juggling with Mr. Fields* (nominated for The Kilroys List); and *Persephone* (Semifinalist: Little Fish Theatre's Pick of the Vine). Her short plays *First Day in Trade* and *The Great Gaffe* are included in *The Best Ten-Minute Plays* 2017 and *The Best Ten-Minute Plays* 2016 (Smith and Kraus). She has worked in publishing, directed literary programs for the YMCA National Writer's Voice and The Academy of American Poets, and is a former producer of the nonprofit Pelham Children's Theater. She lives near New York City with her husband, son, and daughter, two dogs, two cats, and a rabbit.